THE STORY OF

MALALA YOUSAFZAI

A Biography Book for New Readers

Written by
Joan Marie Galat

Illustrated by
Aura Lewis

ROCKRIDGE PRESS

For my very dear friends, Fadila Muslim and Shukri, Huda, Nureddin, Nada, and Yusuf Selmo—the most charming newcomers to Canada from Syria.

For general information on our other products and services or to obtain technical support, please contact our Customer Care Department within the United States at (866) 744-2665, or outside the United States at (510) 253-0500.

Rockridge Press publishes its books in a variety of electronic and print formats. Some content that appears in print may not be available in electronic books, and vice versa.

Series Designer: Angela Navarra

Interior and Cover Designer: Jane Archer

Art Producer: Sue Bischofberger

Editor: Kristen Depken

Production Editor: Mia Moran

Illustrations © 2020 Aura Lewis. Maps courtesy of Creative Market

Photography © dpa picture alliance/Alamy Stock Photo, pp, 47 and 50; SOPA Images Limited/Alamy Stock Photo, p. 49

Author photo courtesy of Rob Hislop Photography

Illustrator photo courtesy of Eugenia Mello

ISBN: Print 978-1-64739-682-4 | eBook 978-1-64739-420-2

R0

Printed in China

CONTENTS

CHAPTER 1

AN ACTIVIST IS BORN

Meet Malala

Malala Yousafzai (you-zahf-SAI) was just 11 years old when going to school became unsafe. **Militants**, called the **Taliban**, had recently brought new laws to her city in Pakistan. Before the Taliban became strong, women and teenage girls could choose whether or not they wanted to wear **burqas**, which are head-to-toe garments with small slits for eyes. Now all women and older girls were forced to wear them. Television and radio were banned. Girls over the age of 10 could not go to school anymore.

Malala was horrified. She loved to read and learn. Her dream was to be a doctor. How could that happen without school? Anyone who broke the rules would be punished. The Taliban carried guns and patrolled the streets. But Malala could not stay silent. She became an **activist**—a person who tries to change things that are unfair.

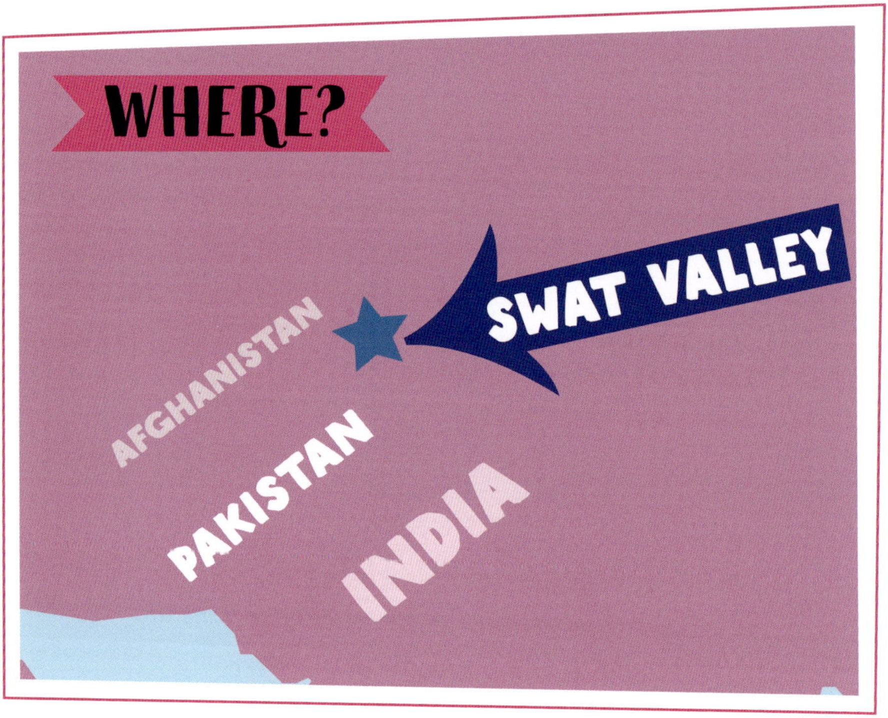

Malala's family is **Muslim**. They practice the religion of **Islam**, which follows a holy book called the **Quran**. When praying to God, they call him by the special name **Allah.** The Taliban were also Muslim, but they were **extremists.** Most people found their beliefs unreasonable.

Malala fought back by giving speeches about why **education** is important for everyone. Other people spoke out, too. Eventually, the Taliban let girls return to classes. But they made a new rule—girls would have to wear burqas. Living under Taliban rule was hard, but Malala continued to demand **justice**.

As you get to know Malala, you will see how bravery made her famous. Around the world, people want to know more about Malala. How did a young girl become an activist? What might she do next?

JUMP –IN THE– THINK TANK

What would your life be like if you couldn't go to school?

Malala's World

Malala Yousafzai was born on July 12, 1997, in Mingora, a city in Pakistan's Swat Valley. Her father's reaction to her birth surprised everyone. He was happy to have a daughter! Many **Pashtuns**—people in Pakistan and Afghanistan who speak **Pashto**—do not celebrate a girl's birth. That's because a daughter is seen as a burden. Parents must guard a daughter's **reputation**. If a girl behaves poorly, her family will lose respect. Sons, however, can get jobs and bring wealth. They can grow up to care for aging parents. When a boy is born, Pashtuns throw a party!

When Malala arrived, her parents could not afford to go to the hospital. Malala's mother, Toor Pekai, gave birth in their two-room home, a place with no bathroom or kitchen. Toor had to cook over a fire on the ground.

When the Yousafzais' neighbors learned the baby was a girl, they felt sorry for Toor. But Malala's father, Ziauddin (zee-ow-DIN), did not think like many Pashtuns. He remembered when Benazir Bhutto became Pakistan's first female **prime minister**. She showed that women could do great things. Ziauddin imagined Malala growing into a strong woman, too. He looked into his daughter's eyes and pictured a great future. Ziauddin felt there was something different about this child.

Though most families treated sons and daughters differently, Ziauddin believed all children should have the same **opportunities**. A teacher, Malala's father ran a school where girls and boys learned together. He inspired Malala to fight against **injustice** when the Taliban pushed its way into Swat Valley.

MYTH & FACT

MYTH: Girls were never allowed to go to school in Pakistan.

FACT: Before the Taliban gained power, Malala and many girls like her were able to go to school.

WHEN?

1988 — Benazir Bhutto becomes prime minister.

1994 — Ziauddin opens his first school.

JULY 12 1997 — Malala is born.

CHAPTER 2

THE EARLY YEARS

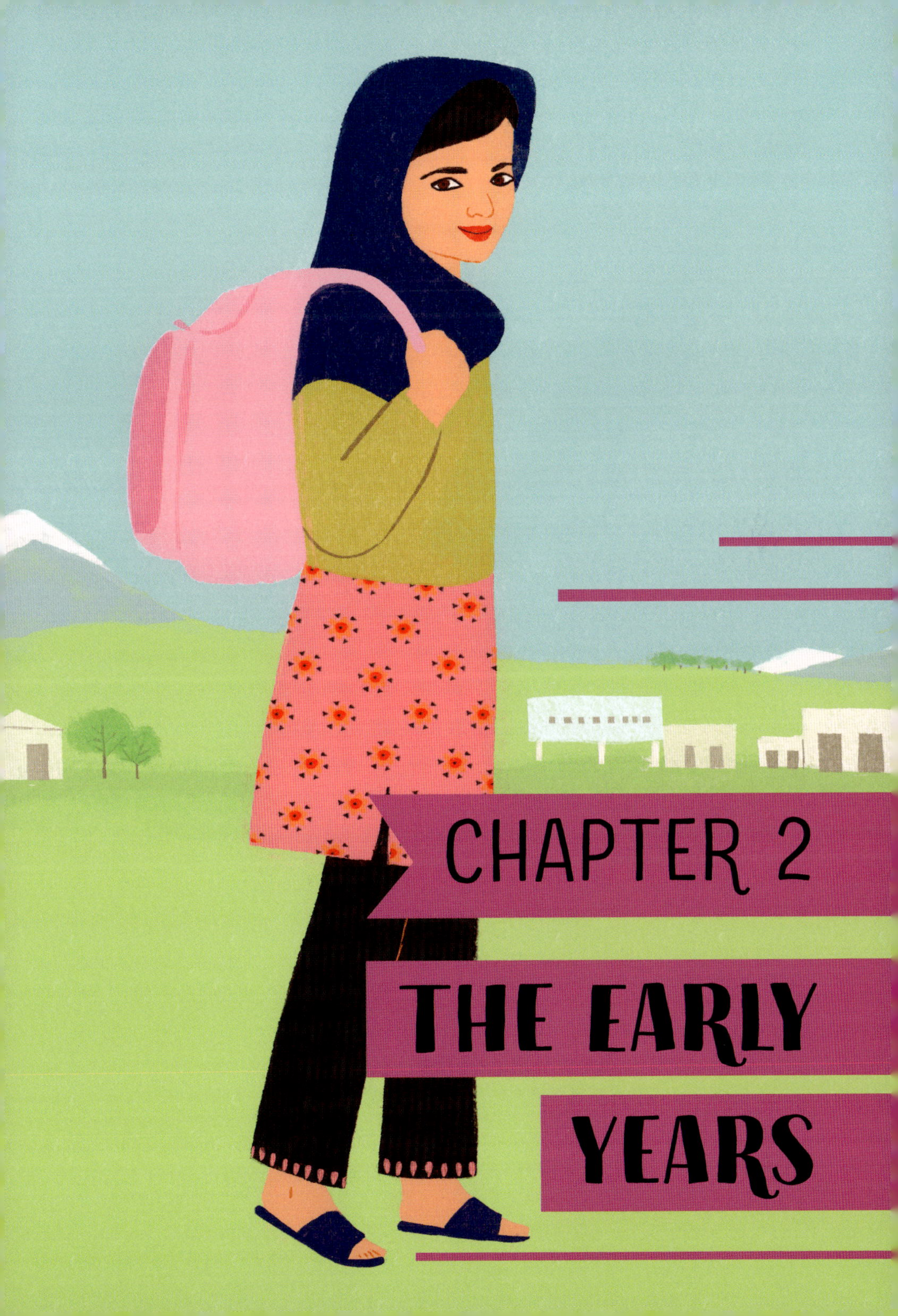

Growing Up in Pakistan

A few months after Malala was born, her family moved into three rooms above Ziauddin's school. Now they had running water. Malala liked visiting the school, even as a toddler. She wandered into classrooms. Sometimes she pretended to be the teacher!

In Malala's early years, she spent most of her time with her mother. Running the school kept Ziauddin busy. Malala's mother could not yet read or write, but she shared Ziauddin's beliefs. She encouraged her daughter to learn.

Malala's home was often filled with guests. She liked having

company. Her mother would spread a long, plastic sheet on the floor. Then she would cover it with food. Ziauddin would read poetry or tell stories about their **ancestors** in the Yousafzai tribe.

Three years after Malala was born, her brother Khushal arrived. Four years later, another brother, Atal, was born.

The Yousafzai Family

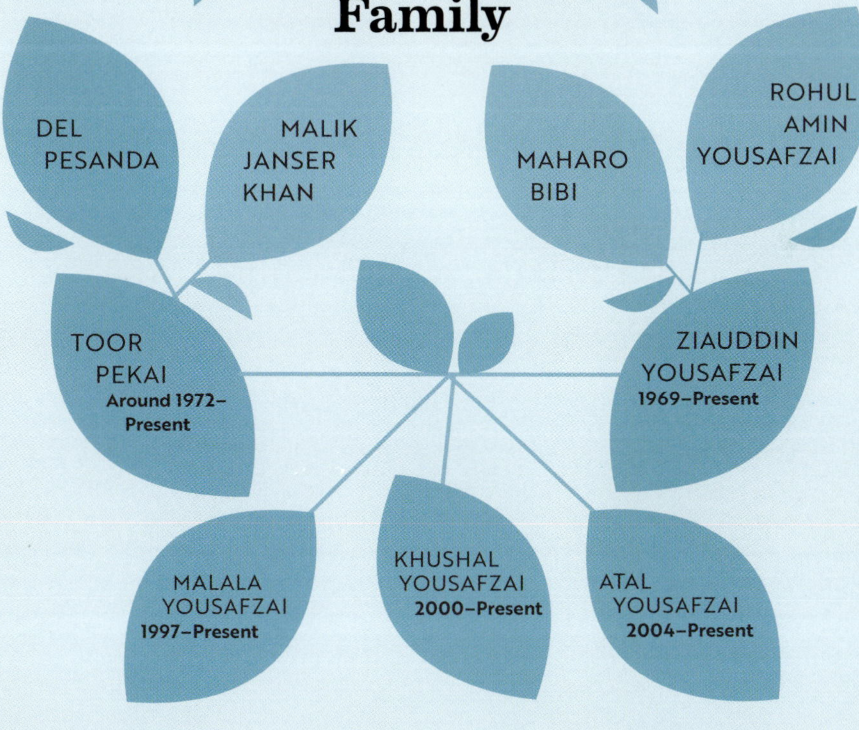

MYTH & FACT

MYTH: All children go to school in Pakistan.

FACT: Some families don't send their daughters to school. Many children cannot attend school because of **poverty**.

A Girl's Life

Malala started school when she was five. She liked to try every activity, from drama to sports, like **badminton**. She worked hard to get good grades, even spending extra time on her hardest subject, math. Malala was determined to be first on the honors list.

When not busy with books, Malala loved to climb onto the flat roof of their home. She gazed at the snow-topped mountains that surrounded Swat Valley. It was a time to daydream. Malala also liked to play **cricket** with her brothers

and neighbors. Sometimes they played on the flat roof, and other times on the street.

On holidays, Malala's family traveled to the villages where her parents grew up. While the women cooked for the men, she played with her cousins. A favorite game was "weddings." The girls pretended to be brides and dressed up with jewelry. Everyone knew some parents arranged marriages for young daughters instead of sending them to school. Many parents saw educating girls as a waste of money. Malala was grateful her father wanted her in school.

When Malala grew older, the village felt less fun. Some of the **traditions** villagers followed were strict. Teenagers had to stay inside. Women

JUMP IN THE THINK TANK

How would you feel if you couldn't do what you want just because you're a boy or a girl?

covered their faces when they went out. They did not speak to men, except for close relatives. Malala thought these traditions were unfair. They meant that, one day, she would not be able to play cricket. She would have to cook for her brothers!

Malala loved Swat Valley, but it was hard not to think about the different rules for girls and boys, and women and men. She wondered if there was a way for everyone to be treated equally.

WHEN?

OCTOBER 1997: The Yousafzai family moves to rooms above the school.

2000: Malala's brother Khushal is born.

2002: Malala starts school.

2004: Malala's brother Atal is born.

CHAPTER 3

DREAMING OF A BETTER WORLD

The Magic Pencil

Eventually, the Yousafzais moved to a different house. They also got a television! On Malala's favorite show, a boy drew pictures with a magic pencil. Anything he drew became real. Malala longed for a magic pencil. She knew exactly who she would use it to help first.

In Swat Valley, people often dumped their trash on empty land. One day, Malala's mother asked her to take some potato peels and eggshells to the dump near their home. Malala

JUMP IN THE THINK TANK

Why is education so important? How can people use a good education to help others?

saw children digging through the garbage. They looked dirty and as if no one took care of them. The children were sorting metal, glass, and paper to sell. Malala felt heartbroken. It was so unfair they had to work. She wished all children could go to school like she did. If only she had a magic pencil!

Malala brought her father to the dump. He tried to speak to the children, but they ran away. She begged Ziauddin to let the children attend his school for free. It was not the first time. Malala and her mother had already convinced him to allow some girls to attend without paying **tuition**.

Like Ziauddin, Malala's mother often helped people. Even though the family did not always have enough money, Toor gave hungry students breakfast. She also visited people in the hospital.

Malala knew it would take more than a magic pencil to truly help. She understood education would be her best tool.

Danger Strikes

Malala was eight years old when her desk began to shake. It was an earthquake, the biggest to ever hit Swat Valley. Hearts trembling, everyone ran outdoors. Finally, the rumbles stopped. Malala and her brothers rushed home to find their mother. Toor cried and hugged her children.

Aftershocks shook the valley into the evening. Ziauddin did not get home until late. His school had grown, and he had to check each building to make sure everything was all right. Malala was glad to hear her father's school was safe, but she was still frightened. Some buildings in Mingora had collapsed. Other areas were worse, with whole villages reduced to rubble. **Landslides** blocked roads and people were stranded. More than a million people lost their homes. Many died and even more were injured. Thousands of schools were destroyed. Malala helped her mother gather blankets. She worked with her classmates to raise money for the victims.

> "There are many problems, but I think there is a solution to all these problems; it's just one, and it's education."

At this time, Pakistan was led

by a **dictator** who did little to help. Local **governments** could not work without buildings or electricity. In the confusion, militant groups tried to take over. They set up hospitals and brought aid to win people over. They also forced harsh extremist views on everyone who lived in Swat Valley. The militants told the villagers that the earthquake was God's punishment for not properly following Islamic law. Malala wondered why the government did not try harder to help. She also wondered what to think of the extremists. Would they make life harder?

WHEN?

Swat Valley's biggest earthquake ever occurs.

OCTOBER 2005

Militant groups rise to power in Swat Valley.

2005 TO 2006

CHAPTER 4

LIVING IN FEAR

Rise of the Taliban

In Mingora, many people were **illiterate**—they could not read or write. The best way to reach them was through radio. Maulana Fazlullah (mau-LAH-nah fahz-loo-LAH), an extremist leader, started a radio station. He said women with too much freedom caused the earthquake. He blamed music, movies, and dancing, too.

Malala watched his followers set fire to TVs, CDs, and DVDs. Fazlullah said God would punish those who didn't listen. Malala asked her father if that was true. He told her Fazlullah was fooling people. Instead of throwing their TV away, Ziauddin hid it in a closet.

The extremists destroyed statues, paintings, and even some board games. One day, Fazlullah announced that girls should not go to school. Malala worried that she would be forced to spend her whole life inside. Ziauddin made a decision.

Even though it was dangerous, he would keep his schools open to boys and girls. Malala was nervous, but she continued to go to class.

At night, the extremists began to destroy schools. They attacked local police forces and took control of Mingora. The government sent troops to fight the extremists. For a short time, Malala felt hopeful. But the extremists came back, now banning computers and books.

On school days, Malala hid her books under her shawl. She kept her head down and hurried

to class, hoping the extremists would not notice her. At night, Malala hid her books under her bed. She worried about what might happen next.

MYTH & FACT

MYTH: Anyone could read the Quran to learn about Islamic law.

FACT: Many people couldn't read. They didn't know the extremists were making up religious laws.

Speaking Up

The extremists joined forces with other militant groups. Now called the Pakistan Taliban, their power grew. More rules roared through the radio.

Activists like Malala's father tried to stop the Taliban. He encouraged students to speak out. Some girls, including 11-year-old Malala, spoke about peace and education on TV. Over time, though, fewer fathers allowed their daughters to do TV interviews. The girls had reached the age for **purdah**, the practice of concealing themselves from men.

Malala was glad her father did not take away her freedom. One of Pakistan's biggest TV stations had invited her to appear. Malala realized her voice had power. Giving interviews gave her hope. Malala thought that if one man on the radio could cause so many problems, one girl should be able to make a change for the better.

Now Malala was an activist, too. She gave her first public speech in 2008. It took place in Peshawar, a city

JUMP IN THE THINK TANK

Why is it important to stand up for your beliefs? What is something important that you've stood up for?

about a three-hour drive southwest. Malala spoke about the Taliban taking away her right to education.

One day, the Taliban said all girls' schools must close. Malala refused to give up. She began to **blog** for the British Broadcasting Corporation (**BBC**). She wrote about what it was like to be female and live under Taliban rule. Her first entry was titled "I Am Afraid."

WHERE?

Malala wrote under the name Gul Makai. Using her own name would have been too risky. Many people admired the blog writer for speaking the truth. Over time, some people realized Malala was the writer. The Taliban figured it out, too.

WHEN?

2007: Fazlullah arrives and extremists take control in Mingora.

2007: The Pakistan government sends troops to Swat Valley.

2008: Malala gives her first public speech in Peshawar.

2009: Girls over 10 years old are no longer allowed to go to school.

2009: Malala writes her first blog entry as Gul Makai.

CHAPTER 5

A VOICE OF HOPE

In Hiding

Eventually, Fazlullah decided to allow girls age 10 and under to go back to class. Malala's teacher, Madam Maryam, still wanted to teach the older girls. She started a secret class inside the regular school. Malala was 11 but pretended to be younger. She wore everyday clothes instead of a uniform and hid her books under her shawl. She tried not to look nervous as she hurried to her secret school.

Living this way made Malala angry. In her blog, she asked why the army did not stop the extremists. Finally, the army decided to take control. First, they told everyone to leave Mingora. Malala did not want to go. She could not stop her tears.

Malala and her family squeezed into friends' and neighbors' cars. The roads were jammed. Nearly a million people were trying to leave

JUMP —IN THE— THINK TANK

What would it be like to leave your home without any warning? How would you feel if war separated your family?

Swat Valley at the same time. Ziauddin went to Peshawar to warn people about what was happening. Malala and the rest of her family headed for Shangla, Ziauddin's family's village. The Yousafzais had become **internally displaced persons**, people who are forced to move from their homes but who stay in their own country.

The army set up roadblocks. Carrying their belongings, Malala, her mother,

and her brothers had to walk 15 miles to Shangla. They stayed with relatives, and Malala was able to go to school again. After classes, she listened to the radio, hoping for good news.

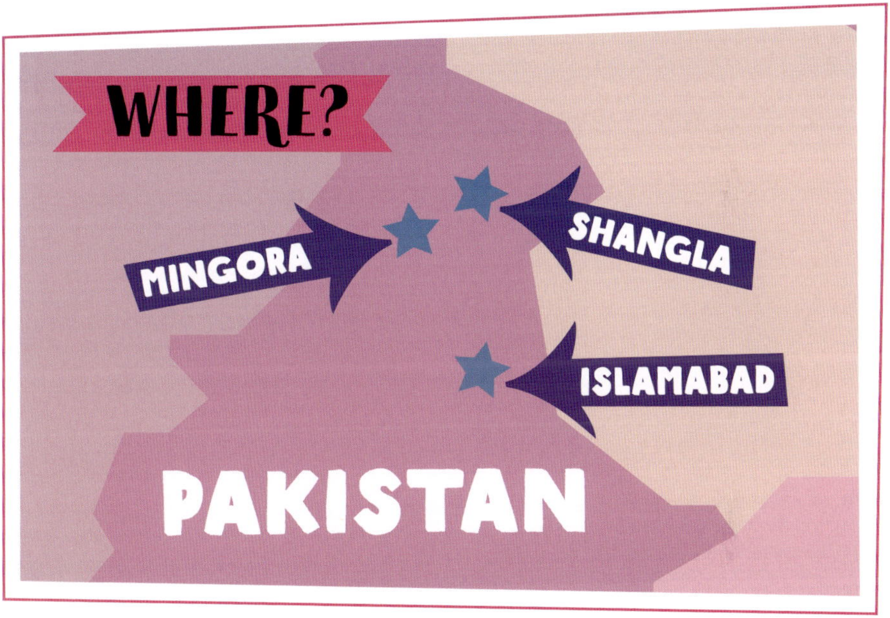

Working for Peace

After almost six weeks in Shangla, Malala got good news. They would go to Peshawar to be with Ziauddin. Finally, Malala could hug her father tight. The family traveled to Islamabad,

Pakistan's **capital**. Richard Holbrooke, an American **ambassador**, would be there for an important meeting. Malala and Ziauddin were invited to the event. This made Malala feel like she could help. She knew Holbrooke had the power to lead change. She asked him to help girls get an education. Holbrooke agreed Pakistan had many problems, but he did not make any promises.

After almost three months, it was safe to return to Mingora. Malala felt sad about the many changes. Buildings had been bombed into rubble. Burned-out cars looked like crusted black shells. The army had set up **checkpoints** on the roads to look for weapons and see who was coming and going. Home felt different than before.

Now 13 years old, Malala and other girls older than 10 could return to school. Even though the army was in charge of Mingora, the Taliban was still a **threat**. Malala continued to talk to

reporters and give speeches. She spoke about education for girls and called for an end to **child labor**, which forced children to work.

> "They cannot stop me.
> I will get my education
> if it's at home, school,
> or somewhere else."

People noticed Malala's **activism**. In 2011, she was given an important award: Pakistan's first National Peace Prize. It came to be known as the Malala Prize.

WHEN?

Malala leaves Mingora.

MAY **2009**

The Taliban leaves Mingora.

JULY **2009**

Malala returns to school.

AUGUST **2009**

Malala wins the Pakistan National Peace Prize.

2011

CHAPTER 6

THE DAY EVERYTHING CHANGED

The Ride Home

The more Malala spoke out, the more attention she received. The Taliban began to make threats against Malala. Her parents wondered if she should stop being an activist. Now 15 years old, Malala refused to quit. Still, she was nervous. Every night, she made sure the doors and outdoor gate were locked. She prayed for a safer world.

One day after school, Atal was supposed to ride the school bus home with his sister but decided to walk instead. Malala waited for the bus with her friends. She was enjoying their time together. They had just taken an exam and Malala felt good about her answers.

When the bus arrived, Malala sat with her friend, Moniba, near the back. The bus turned at an army checkpoint. Usually there was traffic, but today the road seemed quiet. The bus pulled to a sudden stop. Malala could not see what was happening.

Two men with guns had forced the bus to stop. They climbed aboard and asked which girl was Malala. No one spoke, but their eyes turned to Malala. After that, Malala could not remember what happened. Everything went blank. When Malala woke up, she was in a hospital in the United Kingdom, more than 5,000 miles away!

> "I know the importance of education because my pens and books were taken from me by force."

Fighting for Life

Malala had been attacked by the Taliban. No one knew if she would survive. She was flown to a hospital for special treatment in the city of Birmingham, in England. When Malala woke

up, everyone was speaking English. Unable to talk, she wrote on a piece of paper. She wanted to know where her father was, and if she had been shot! She wanted to know where she was. Doctors and nurses explained what happened. They were kind, but Malala wanted her family. Back in Pakistan, Ziauddin needed to get **passports** and other paperwork to travel. After 10 days, Malala's family arrived.

Around the world, people showed Malala how much they cared. They sent thousands of cards, as well as flowers, toys, and other presents.

Leaders, **politicians**, movie stars, and famous singers wrote to Malala. The **United Nations** made November 10 Malala Day. Hundreds of reporters came to the hospital to see how she was doing. One of her caregivers, Dr. Fiona, gave her a white teddy bear. Malala named it Lily.

JUMP IN THE THINK TANK

How did Malala's story become so well-known? Why do you think so many people wrote to her?

Malala's recovery would take time. A brain injury meant she would have to learn to talk and walk again. Malala

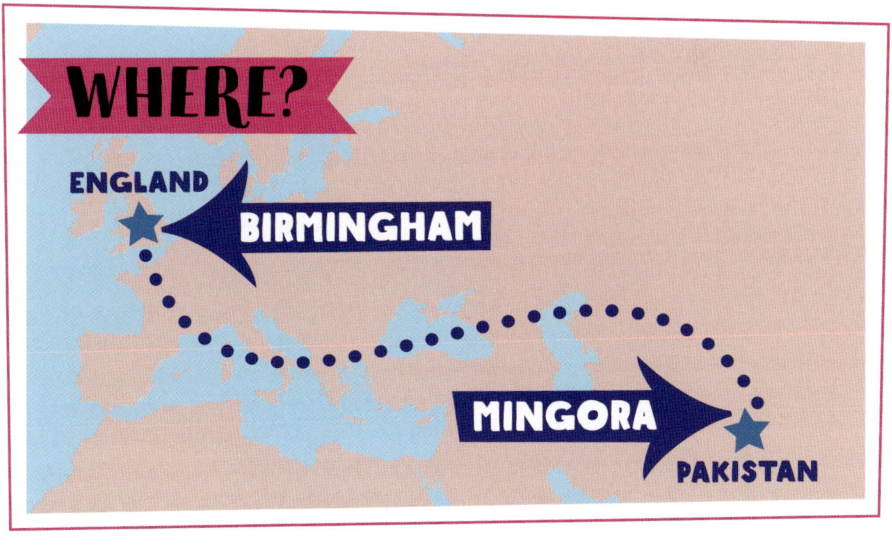

worked in a gym, doing exercises to make her body strong. Finally, Malala was well enough to leave the hospital. She was much stronger, but there would be more **surgeries** ahead. Malala was determined to get better. Instead of being angry about what had happened to her, Malala forgave the man who shot her. She felt God let her live so that she could continue to help others.

WHEN?

The Taliban attacks Malala.	Malala is flown to a hospital in Birmingham.	Malala wakes up in the hospital.	Malala is well enough to leave the hospital.
OCTOBER 9 **2012**	OCTOBER 15 **2012**	OCTOBER 16 **2012**	JANUARY **2013**

CHAPTER 7

A NEW LIFE

Stronger Than Ever

Malala and her family moved to a house with a grassy yard and trees. Life in Birmingham was safer for Malala, but it did not feel like home. Many houses looked the same. None were built of stone and mud, and they had pointed roofs instead of flat ones where you could play cricket. Without old friends dropping in, Malala found it too quiet.

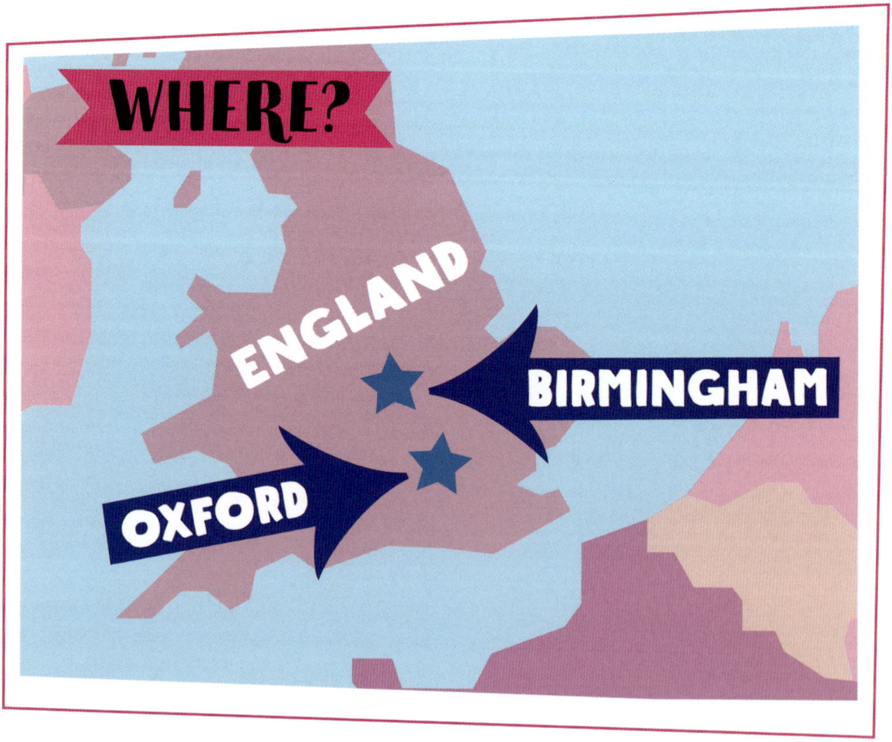

Malala noticed women in England could hold jobs and choose what to wear. Girls could go to school. Rules were the same for everyone and order was kept without scaring people. These things gave Malala hope.

Between doctor appointments, Malala worked on healing and growing stronger. She video-chatted with her friends in Mingora. Malala missed Swat Valley and asked her father when they could go home. Ziauddin told her she needed to heal more. He made excuses because the Taliban was still a threat. Malala realized they would not be going home.

In April 2013, Malala was well enough to start school. She liked being able to go to classes without feeling afraid. Still, Malala felt different from girls raised in England. It was often a lonely time. She reminded herself that getting the best education would make it easier for her to help people. Malala continued to speak out for others.

JUMP
-IN THE-
THINK
TANK

Why do you think the Taliban's attempt to silence Malala made her voice stronger?

Education for All

On Malala's 16th birthday, she was invited to speak at the United Nations in New York. It was a great honor. In her speech, Malala asked world leaders to provide education to all children. They gave her a **standing ovation**. At age 17, Malala won an even more **prestigious** honor when she became the youngest person in the world to receive the **Nobel Peace Prize**.

"I tell my story not because it is unique, but because it is the story of many girls."

Malala used prize money to open schools for girls. She started a **charitable foundation**, called the Malala Fund, to fight for girls' education. She also gave speeches, wrote books, appeared on TV, and visited **refugee camps**. The Taliban had not silenced Malala. Instead, it made her voice stronger.

At the age of 20, Malala began attending Oxford University in the United Kingdom. She studied **philosophy**, **politics**, and **economics**.

Malala found university exciting. There were clubs to join and new friends to meet. Malala still missed Mingora, though.

Then a wonderful thing happened. After more than five years away, Malala was able to return to Mingora for a visit. More than 500 friends and relatives came to see her. She called it the happiest day of her life.

Back at Oxford, Malala continued her studies and **graduated** in June 2020. No matter what career she chooses, she knows she will continue being an activist. The invitations she receives from around the globe show other people care about education, too. Malala knows there is more work to do, but she believes that with many voices joining hers, change will happen. She hopes that one day all girls will have choices about how to live their lives.

WHEN?

JULY 2013 — Malala speaks at the United Nations on her 16th birthday.

2014 — Malala wins the Nobel Peace Prize.

2017 — Malala begins studies at Oxford University.

2018 — Malala visits Pakistan.

2020 — Malala graduates from Oxford University.

CHAPTER 8

SO...WHO IS MALALA YOUSAFZAI?

Challenge Accepted!

Now you know many interesting facts about Malala and her life. Let's check your new knowledge in a little who, what, when, where, why, and how quiz. It's fun to see what you can remember on your own, but if you're stuck, flip back to look up the answers.

1 Who is Malala?

→ A An activist
→ B An author
→ C A public speaker
→ D All of the above

2 Where was Malala born?

→ A Birmingham
→ B Mingora
→ C Peshawar
→ D Shangla

3 When was Malala born?

- A July 12, 1997
- B September 11, 2001
- C January 15, 2009
- D July 12, 2013

4 Why did Malala become an activist?

- A To avoid her brothers
- B To get out of school
- C To give girls the same opportunities as boys
- D To talk to reporters

5 Who made threats against Malala?

- A The Taliban
- B Teachers
- C Neighbors
- D Pakistan's army

6 **When did Malala become an internally displaced person?**

- A 1997
- B 2009
- C 2011
- D 2019

7 **Why is Malala a role model?**

- A For doing well in school
- B For skateboard tricks
- C For standing up for children's rights
- D For helping her mother

8 **How has Malala spread her message?**

- A By blogging and writing books
- B By speaking to politicians
- C By giving media interviews
- D All of the above

9 How old was Malala when she spoke at the United Nations?

- A 100
- B 20
- C 16
- D 14

10 What has Malala accomplished?

- A Inventing a magic pencil
- B Competing in the Olympics
- C Saving whales
- D Becoming the youngest person to win the Nobel Peace Prize

Answer Key: 1. D; 2. B; 3. A; 4. C; 5. A; 6. B; 7. C; 8. D; 9. C; 10. D

Our World

Malala's voice has helped make a difference in the world. Let's see some of the changes her work inspired.

→ Thanks to Malala's activism, children and adults around the world are talking about children's education and looking for solutions. Malala has inspired others to share their stories, become activists, and not give up. Kids are seeing that you can speak out, no matter how old you are.

→ Malala believes peace begins with one's own life. By forgiving the man who shot her, Malala is an inspiration to everyone who has suffered from another person's actions.

→ Inspired by Malala, Gordon Brown, a United Nations **envoy** for Global Education, started the Malala **petition**. It asked the United Nations to recommit to its goal for all children to go to school. More than three million people signed the petition. This led Pakistan to pass a new law in 2012. It gives free education to children ages 5 to 16 in Pakistan.

JUMP IN THE THINK TANK FOR MORE!

Imagine living a life like Malala's and think about how her actions have changed the world.

→ Knowing what Malala achieved, do you think age matters if you want to make a difference? Why or why not?

→ How is Malala's goal to end child labor connected to education?

→ How does knowing about Malala's life make you feel about school? What might happen if you don't get a complete education?

Glossary

activism: The act of trying to change things that are unfair

activist: A person who tries to change things that are unfair

aftershocks: Small earthquakes that happen after a larger earthquake

Allah: God's name in Islam

ambassador: A high-ranking person in government who represents that person's government in other countries

ancestors: A person's parents, grandparents, and other older relatives going back in history

badminton: A sport played with a racket that is used to hit a shuttlecock over a net

BBC: The British Broadcasting Corporation, which is a large media company that broadcasts through radio, television, and the Internet

blog: A website where a writer shares opinions, information, and personal stories

burqa: A veil that covers a female's head and body, leaving only a small slit for the eyes

capital: The city where a country's top government is located

charitable foundation: An organization that helps others

checkpoints: Places, such as roadblocks, where authorities check for weapons and see who is coming and going

child labor: The illegal use of children as workers

cricket: A team sport played with a ball and bat

dictator: A ruler who obtains power by force

economics: The science of money, goods, and services

education: Formal schooling

envoy: A messenger or representative

extremists: People who hold beliefs that are considered extreme or unreasonable

government: The system of rules and people that manage a country, state, city, or local community

graduated: Completed studies at a school or university

illiterate: Unable to read or write

injustice: An act or behavior that's not fair, right, or equal

internally displaced persons: People forced to move from their homes, but who remain in their own country

Islam: A religion that believes in Allah and follows a holy book called the Quran

justice: Fairness

landslide: The fast movement of a mass of rock or earth down a slope

militants: People involved in warfare

Muslim: A person who follows the religion of Islam

Nobel Peace Prize: An international prize awarded every year for outstanding work in the promotion of peace

opportunities: Situations where success is possible

Pashto: An Iranian language spoken by Pashtuns

Pashtuns: People in Pakistan or Afghanistan who speak Pashto

passports: Documents used when traveling to prove a person's identity and citizenship

petition: A written request made to an organization or government

philosophy: The study of ideas about knowledge, including what is right and wrong

politicians: People whose jobs involve making decisions to run a government

politics: Activities related to the government of a city, state, or country

poverty: The state of being very poor

prestigious: Important and admirable

prime minister: The top leader in a country

purdah: The practice of teenage girls and women staying hidden from men

Quran: A book containing sacred writings used by Muslims

refugee camps: Temporary places to live, for people escaping danger

reporters: People who gather and report news

reputation: Other peoples' opinion about a person's behavior or character

standing ovation: When people stand up to clap for someone

surgeries: Medical treatments that involve repairing damage to the body

Taliban: A militant group with extreme ideas about Islamic law

threat: Something intended to cause harm

traditions: Beliefs or activities in a culture that continue from one generation to the next

tuition: Money given to a school to pay for instruction

United Nations: A political organization of member countries from around the world that works for peace and cooperation among nations

Bibliography

CNN Library. "Malala Yousafzai Fast Facts." Last modified July 5, 2019. CNN.com/2015/08/20/world/malala-yousafzai-fast-facts/index.html.

CTV News. "Malala's Impact, Two Years After Her Shooting." Last modified October 10, 2014. CTVNews.ca/world/malala-s-impact-two-years-after-her-shooting-1.2048562.

Dias, Chelsea. "10 Ways Malala Yousafzai Has Changed the World." Mic. July 23, 2013. Mic.com/articles/55333/10-ways-malala-yousafzai-has-changed-the-world.

Encyclopaedia Britannica. "Malala Yousafzai." Last modified April 24, 2020. Britannica.com/biography/Malala-Yousafzai.

Hai Kakar, Abdul. "Meet the Family Behind Malala." *The Atlantic*. November 7, 2013. TheAtlantic.com/international/archive/2013/11/meet-the-family-behind-malala/281257.

Harris, Alex. "Top 3 Ways Malala Has Changed the World." Plan International UK. July 12, 2016. Plan-UK.org/blogs/thanks-to-malala.

Malala Fund. Accessed March 24, 2020. Malala.org.

The New Humanitarian. "Timeline on Swat Valley Turbulence." February 11, 2009. TheNewHumanitarian.org/feature/2009/02/11/timeline-swat-valley-turbulence.

UNESCO. "UNESCO Malala Fund for Girls' Right to Education." Accessed March 23, 2020. en.UNESCO.org/themes/education-and-gender-equality/malala-fund.

Washington Times. "Taliban Bans Education for Girls in Swat Valley." January 5, 2009. WashingtonTimes.com/news/2009/jan/5/taliban-bans-education-for-girls-in-pakistans-swat.

We Can End Poverty: Millennium Development Goals and Beyond 2015 (United Nations website). "Goal 2: Achieve Universal Primary Education." Accessed March 19, 2020. UN.org/millenniumgoals/education.shtml.

Yousafzai, Malala, and Christina Lamb. *I Am Malala: The Girl Who Stood Up for Education and Was Shot by the Taliban*. New York: Little, Brown and Company, 2013.

Yousafzai, Malala, and Liz Welch. *We Are Displaced: My Journey and Stories from Refugee Girls around the World*. New York: Little, Brown and Company, 2019.

Yousafzai, Ziauddin, and Louise Carpenter. *Let Her Fly: A Father's Journey*. New York: Little, Brown and Company, 2018.

Acknowledgments

Thanks to Malala Yousafzai for living a courageous and inspirational life, especially when facing hardship and tragedy. In becoming a public figure who generously and genuinely shares her experiences with the world, she has enabled others to take courage, grow, and join in standing up for children's rights and education for girls. I also acknowledge Malala's parents—Toor Pekai and Ziauddin—for creating a home environment where it is normal and safe for a daughter to explore her own potential, even when cultural traditions make this path challenging. Thanks to my husband, Grant Wiens, who makes my life easier in every way so that I can focus on the writing projects that call to me. Hearty thanks also to my talented editor, Kristen Depken, for her knowledge and sound insights, along with Matt Buonaguro and the other professionals who make up the Callisto Media team.

—J.M.G.

About the Author

JOAN MARIE GALAT began writing books at the age of nine but was not published until age 12, when she became a paid weekly newspaper columnist. Now she is the author of more than 20 books for children and adults. Her titles include a Canadian national bestseller, translations into five languages, and numerous awards including a Crystal Kite. She is a recipient of the Martha Weston Grant, awarded annually to one worldwide member of the Society of Children's Book Writers and Illustrators (SCBWI).

As well as writing about inspiring people, Joan loves to explore science and the natural world. She shares her love of the stars in the Dot to Dot in the Sky series (Whitecap Books), which combines astronomy with the ancient myths that give night-sky objects their names. Joan encourages people to turn out the lights for wildlife in *Dark Matters: Nature's Reaction to Light Pollution* (Red Deer Press) and inspires readers to get creative in *Solve This! Wild and Wacky Challenges for the Genius Engineer in You* (National Geographic Kids).

A freelance writer, editor, and corporate trainer, Joan operates MoonDot Media (MoonDotMedia.com). Her freelance work includes writing speeches, magazine articles, and even a cartoon! When not tapping on her keyboard, Joan loves to spend time outdoors, enjoy the night sky, walk on stilts, and travel. Public speaking has taken her across Canada and internationally, including to a United Nations Environment Programme event in South Korea. Visit **JoanGalat.com** to find out more about Joan's books and ask about school presentations, available both in person and through video chat.

About the Illustrator

AURA LEWIS is an author-illustrator with an MFA from the School of Visual Arts in New York City. Her work is featured in books for children and adults, TV titles, stationery, and editorial publications. Aura is inspired by fashion and culture from all over the world, playful color, vintage design, and social activism.